COLOURFUL AUSTRALIA
SYDNEY

Produced by
Ted Smart & David Gibbon

Featuring the Photography of
Neil Sutherland & Eberhard Streichan

Published by Colour Library Books for
GORDON & GOTCH LTD

ARAFURA SEA

TIMOR
SEA

INDIAN
OCEAN

CORAL SEA

Torres Strait

DARWIN

Arnhem Land

Cape
York
Peninsula

GULF OF
CARPENTARIA

Kimberley
Plateau

NORTHERN

TERRITORY

Barkly Tableland

Cairns

GREAT BARRIER REEF

Great Sandy
Desert

Townsville

Cloncurry ○   ○ Richmond ○

Mackay ●

○ The Granites

QUEENSLAND

Macdonnell Ranges

Rockhampton ●

Gibson Desert

○ Alice Springs

GREAT DIVIDING RANGE

WESTERN

AUSTRALIA

△ Ayers Rock   Simpson Desert

Bundaberg ●

Shark
Bay

Lake Eyre Basin

Charleville ○

Great Victoria
Desert

Lake Eyre

Grey
Range

Toowoomba ○   Ipswich ○   BRISB ●

Geraldton ○

SOUTH
AUSTRALIA

NEW SOUTH
WALES

○ Kalgoorlie

Nullarbor Plain

Flinders
Range

PERTH ●
Fremantle ○

Port Pirie ○

Broken Hill ○

Maitland ○
Newcastle ○

Elizabeth ○

SYDNEY ●

ADELAIDE ●

Wollongong ○

Spencer
Gulf

CANBERRA ●

VICTORIA

SOUTH AUSTRALIAN BASIN

Ballarat ○   MELBOURNE ●

Geelong ○

TASMAN
SEA

Bass Strait

TASMANIA   ○ Launceston

Queenstown ○

Hobart ●

TITLES IN THE COLOURFUL AUSTRALIA SERIES
Animals of Australia
Wild Flowers of Australia
Perth
Koalas
Melbourne
Tasmania
Adelaide
Brisbane
Canberra
Sydney
Ayers Rock and the Olgas
The Great Barrier Reef
The Outback

Published in Australia by Gordon & Gotch Ltd.

First published in Great Britain 1984 by Colour Library Books Ltd.
© 1984 Illustrations and text: Colour Library Books Ltd.,
Guildford, Surrey, England.
Colour separations by Llovet, Barcelona, Spain.
Printed and bound by Gráficas Estella, Spain.
All rights reserved.

ISBN 0 86283 137 7

Sydney bursts upon the visitor in an array of unexpected colour and vitality. Most people know of the Opera House and the Harbour Bridge, but very few are prepared for the majesty of their setting. Resplendent against the azure blue of the harbour or the twinkling city lights, they take on a totally unexpected beauty and elegance. The city itself is throbbing with life. The broad shopping streets of the city centre and the rich variety of cultures and influences are unmatched anywhere else in Australia. Indeed, Sydney is the only truly cosmopolitan city on the continent, having established trade links with China, America and Britain in its very earliest days, and is the the first port of call for most visitors to this wonderful country.

Sydneysiders, as they call themselves, know well how to enjoy their city. They are a remarkable people, being hardy, sophisticated, but above all, easy-going and relaxed in their attitudes. The sub-tropical climate of their city is an open invitation to those who enjoy outdoor sports, and that includes almost everyone in Sydney. There are tennis-courts, numerous parks and, perhaps most important of all, beaches. The typical Australian, and Sydneysiders are no exception, have fallen in love with beach life; indeed their whole culture may appear to be influenced by it. Long hours spent on the beach, soaking up the sunshine and watching the beautiful 'Sheilas' go by, interspersed with bursts of activity surfing or swimming is an integral part of the Sydneysider's life style. For those more interested in culture there are numerous concerts and plays put on throughout the city and, of course, there is the Opera House. Overlooking the Harbour, the graceful sweep of the Opera House's roof covers performances of the world's greatest operas, staged in lavish style as befits such a masterpiece of architecture.

This great city began life almost by accident. In 1770, after a long and arduous voyage, Captain Cook came across the long sought *Terra Australis Incognita*. Sailing north along the coast, he discovered and named many important coastal features. Among them was a large bay where he and his crew were astounded by the variety and beauty of the plant life. He named it Botany Bay. After sailing along the entire eastern coast of the continent, Cook returned home with his report on the new land. These reports were so impressive that the government decided to act upon them.

Consequently, eighteen years later, Captain Arthur Phillip was sent off with a fleet of ships, convicts, marines and orders to found a penal colony at Botany Bay. However, when Captain Phillip reached the proposed site of the new colony he found that it was entirely unsuitable; the land was unproductive and the bay could not protect his ships. So Captain Phillip decided to move the colony to another location, but first he had to find somewhere. One of the places that he explored was a bay that Captain Cook had named Port Jackson. Captain Phillip described it as "the finest harbour in the world, in which a thousand sail of the line may ride in the most perfect security." He set up his settlement on the shores of a small inlet, which he called Sydney Cove and which remains the main terminal for passenger liners to this day.

It was not long before people began to pour into the new settlement. First came convicts and then free settlers, trying to clear farms and make a livelihood from the untamed soil. The harsh days of early Sydney are recreated a short drive away, to the north of the modern city. Old Sydney Town stands on the Pacific Highway, near Gosford. Here cottages, convict huts, workshops and a replica ship have been constructed to recreate the look and atmosphere of the first European settlement on the continent. The town has been fully staffed with soldiers, convicts and craftsmen who act the parts of the original inhabitants.

By 1821, under the leadership of Governer Macquarie, Sydney had become bustling and respectable with hospitals, churches, schools and parks scattered throughout the town. The harsh days of the convict transportations were soon left far behind as Sydney grew to be the most important financial centre and largest city on the continent: by 1900 almost half a million people lived in Sydney. For a few years Sydney was overtaken in importance by Melbourne, but today it has reassumed its place as the first city in Australia.

The city of Sydney, in the closing years of this century, extends across 700 square miles of New South Wales and has a population in excess of three million. The tremendous area is due to the desire of every Australian to own his own home. Throughout the suburbs, Sydney is a city of wide streets and low bungalows. It is only in the heart of the city that tall skyscrapers rise and even here imaginative architecture and a sensible approach have created an appealing and cohesive whole, reflecting the city's dynamism and energy.

The undisputed playground of Sydney is the suburb of Manly. The beaches and facilities here are hard to match, while the climate is ideal. The cove earned its name in the time of Captain Phillip. He was impressed by the proud bearing of the local Aborigines and so named the area Manly. The bathing and surfing is so much a part of the suburb that it is strange to think that there was once a time when such activities were illegal. In 1838 a law was passed which banned public bathing between 6 am and 8 pm. By 1902, it was clear that Manly's major asset was being ruined by this law and a local newspaperman decided to force the issue. Mr. W H Gocher announced that he would bathe in public every day, and nobody arrested him. From that time on the beaches of Manly became increasingly popular, establishing a tradition that is truly Australian. Another great invention came to the area with a gardener called Tommy Tanner, who hailed from the South Sea Islands. Much to the surprise of the locals Tommy would throw himself into the largest waves and ride them to the shore. It wasn't long before someone thought of doing it on a plank of wood, and surfing was born.

Commercial hub of the South Pacific, Sydney is a capital city in all but name – it is the cultural and industrial centre of a rapidly expanding nation.

Pages 2 and 3 an unusual view of the Opera House and Harbour Bridge. *Previous pages* the city from the Sydney Tower, which stands some 325 metres tall. The nineteenth century has left many fine buildings to present-day Sydney. The Town Hall *right* was completed in 1874 and was constructed in the style of an Italian Renaissance palace. Saint Mary's Roman Catholic Cathedral *above,* however, was finished nine years earlier and looked for its inspiration to the great Gothic masterpieces of northern Europe. The Strand Arcade *top and opposite page* protects many small shops from the elements. *Overleaf* an aerial view of the city from the west.

Previous pages the busy,
traffic-bound streets of
central Sydney. *These pages*
some of the more famous
sights of Sydney. *Overleaf*
is a magnificent aerial
view of the city centre.

Previous pages the famous Sydney Opera House which stands on Bennelong Point, overlooking the Harbour. The buildings of old and new Sydney contrast with each other and yet seem to form a cohesive whole. Some examples of the differing styles are shown on these pages: the Conservatorium of Music *below* and the Bahai Temple *left*, the Sydney Tower *opposite page*, the Opera House *above* and the Botanic Gardens *above left. Overleaf* can be seen the many faces of Sydney Harbour.

Left, top and opposite page, bottom is shown the Harbour Bridge. Other landmarks of the city are: *above* the El Alamein Fountain and *opposite page, top* the recently restored Pier One.

Previous pages the Opera House and the city by night. Sydney's early trading links with Britain, America and the Far East gave it a cosmopolitan air. Today, Chinatown *these* *pages* is a noted nightspot with its collection of restaurants and bars. *Overleaf* a shopping arcade at the Pacific coast town of Bondi.

Sydneysiders have a great variety of open spaces to visit: *left* the Botanic Gardens, *above* the Phillip fountain, *above left* ANZAC gardens, *top* the giant chess set in Hyde Park, *opposite page, bottom* the El Alamein Fountain in Kings Cross and *opposite page, top* Macquarie Street. *Overleaf* the Opera House, which cost some 102 million dollars to complete.

Previous pages a twilight view of the Harbour Bridge and the Opera House. Much of the old Sydney survives amid the modern, concrete city: *above* Cadman's Cottage and *left and top* Argyle Terrace, both to be found in The Rocks. This area of the city stands complete with pubs and narrow streets, almost as it was when first built. *Opposite page, top* a magnificent view of the city from the Harbour Bridge. *Overleaf* the city from above Walsh Bay, whose docks can be seen in the foreground.

Previous pages the sailing ship *New Endeavour*. The Sydney Tower Centrepoint *above, right and opposite page, bottom* dominates the skyline of the city. Inside the Centrepoint there are shops on three levels. The Tower itself houses two revolving restaurants. *Overleaf* Cockatoo Island in Sydney Harbour.

A view of the city from the Victoria Road at Wrights Point can be seen *previous pages*. Manly Beach *top, right, opposite page, bottom and opposite page, top*, is one of the finest and most popular of Sydney's surfing grounds.

The beach was given its name by Captain Phillip in 1788 because he was so impressed by the masculinity of the local Aborigines. *Overleaf* can be seen Bondi Beach, perhaps the most famous of all Australian beaches.

The seaward coasts *right and opposite page* provide surfing beaches, while the bays *above and top* give calm waters for many of the Sydneysiders' yachts. *Overleaf* some of Sydney's older private houses.

Previous pages sailing is a Sydney passion. Taronga Park Zoo contains many species native to Australia including: *opposite page* the Tasmanian devil *top left*, the cassowary *centre left*, the echidna *centre right*, the kangaroo *bottom left* and *this page right*, the emu *top left*, the koala *top right* and the dingo *above*. Non-Australian animals include: *opposite page top right* the peacock and *bottom right* the brown bear. *Overleaf* can be seen a view of the Harbour. *Pages 62 and 63* a view of Sydney from the southwest.